MACHINE CLOSE-UP

MODERN WARSHIPS & SUBMARINES

David West and Alex Pang

This edition published in 2013 by Wayland

Wayland
Hachette Children's Books
338 Euston Road
London NW1 3BH

Wayland Australia
Level 17/207 Kent Street
Sydney, NSW 2000

Produced by
David West Children's Books
7 Princeton Court
55 Felsham Road
London SW15 1AZ

Copyright © 2013 David West Children's Books

Designer: Gary Jeffrey
Illustrator: Alex Pang
Editor: Katharine Pethick
Consultant: Steve Parker

A CIP catalogue record for this book is available
from the British Library.

ISBN: 9780750278645

2 4 6 8 10 9 7 5 3 1

Printed in China

Wayland is a division of
Hachette Children's Books,
an Hachette UK company.
www.hachette.co.uk

PHOTO CREDITS :
Abbreviations: t-top, m-middle, b-bottom, r-right,
l-left, c-centre.
4-5, PH3 ALTA I. CUTLER; USN; 8b, junmon603; 9tl,
Bundesarchiv; 9b, DoD photo by Petty Officer 3rd Class
Christopher Mobley, U.S. Navy; 30t, U.S. Navy Photo;
30l, MC1 Brien Aho, U.S. Navy Photographer; 30b, U.S.
Navy Photo

CONTENTS

INTRODUCTION

Modern warships and submarines are packed with the most amazing pieces of war hardware and software. From ground-hugging, submarine-launched cruise missiles to 5,000 rounds-a-minute Gatling guns, these are the most expensive of all weapons of war.

WARSHIP FLEET
A parade of modern warships shows the usual ship types in a warship fleet. The aircraft carriers are the capital ships which are protected by frigates and destroyers and unseen attack submarines.

HOW THIS BOOK WORKS

MAIN TEXT

Explains the history of the ship and outlines its primary role.

SPECS

This panel gives information about the ship's speed, dimensions and personnel.

MAIN CUTAWAY

This exploded illustration shows the internal structure of the ship and gives information on the positions of its various working parts.

STEALTH CORVETTE

The Visby is the latest class of corvette to be adopted by the Swedish navy. Corvettes are small, manoeuvrable, lightly armed warships. The Visby's angular design uses stealth technology to create a 'low visibility' presence and its reduced radar signature gives an advantage over enemy ships. All Visby's functions can be hidden behind panels to enable it to keep the smoothest shape possible.

57MM BOFORS GUN
This automatic gun fires up to 220 rounds a minute. The barrel is fully retracted inside the gun casing to reduce its radar signature when not in use.

Pop-up weapons director

Weather sensors

BRIDGE
The high bridge is equipped with an advanced command, control and digital communications system.

ANTI-MINE ROV
Two Remotely Operated underwater Vehicles (ROVs) can detect and dispose of mines safely, ahead of the ship.

ASW grenade launchers

Bow thrusters

VISBY

Helipad

Saab Double Eagle remote operated mine seeker

Sonar array

Tether mount

RBS 15 MkII launcher

ASW torpedo tubes

WEAPONS
The Visby uses sea skimming, 'fire and forget' missiles, fired from concealed launchers. Anti-Submarine Warfare (ASW) capability includes homing torpedoes launched from fixed tubes in the stern. The Visby also carries grenades and depth charges.

RBS 15 Mk II anti-ship missile

Computer guidance

Warhead

Turbojet engine

400mm anti-sub torpedo

Propeller

HULL
The hull is made of layers of carbon fibre and vinyl around a plastic core. This material is strong but light, provides good shock resistance and has a low radar signature.

K31

Superstructure

Anti-radar paint

VISBY CLASS CORVETTE
Crew: 43
Length: 72.6 metres
Beam: 10.4 metres
Top speed: 40 knots (87 kilometres per hour)

COmbined Diesel Or Gas engine system

Two MTU Friedrichshafen 16V 2000 N90 diesel engines

Four Vericor TF50A gas turbines

Kamewa waterjets

ENGINES
CODOG systems use one diesel engine and one geared gas turbine for each propeller/water jet. The diesel engine maintains cruising speed with the gas turbine used for high speed dashes. For maximum power output, the Visby's propulsion system contains two gas turbines for each shaft. CODOG fuel consumption is very high.

INTERESTING FEATURES

This box contains a detailed illustration of the engine or another design feature that makes the ship unique. Informative text explains the feature's function.

EQUIPMENT

Smaller illustrations look in detail at the weapons and other equipment carried by the ship to fulfill its different roles.

RAIDERS AND TRADERS

Warships probably first came about when pirates began raiding merchant ships. Special fast, slim ships with armed men onboard were sent to protect valuable trade routes at sea.

BIREME
The leading warship of the 8th century, the bireme had two banks of oars. Other galleys had up to five banks of oars.

GALLEYS

In the time of Ancient Greece and the Roman Empire, the most common type of warship was the galley – a long, narrow vessel powered by banks of oarsmen. Carrying armed men, it could ram and sink enemy vessels, or come alongside the enemy and attack them. Viking longships were ideal for raiding coastal waters due to their shallow draft.

VIKING LONGSHIP

VENETIAN GALLEY
Fighting galleys were used well into the 16th century in the Mediterranean.

TUDOR FLAGSHIP
The Mary Rose was a 16th century carrack that carried 91 guns.

SAILS AND CANNONS

By the 15th century, warships were carrying cannons. Carracks were large, three or four-masted ocean-going ships. These evolved into speedy galleons – purpose built warships that dominated sea battles.

GALLEON
The Spanish galleon (right) was the ultimate man-o'-war during the early 17th century.

SHIPS OF THE LINE

From the 17th century, warships carried large numbers of cannon on each side. Ships formed a line of battle to fire at each other's broadsides – the tactic that gave them their name. These ships of the line carried up to 140 guns on two or three decks.

The fleets with the heaviest broadsides usually won.

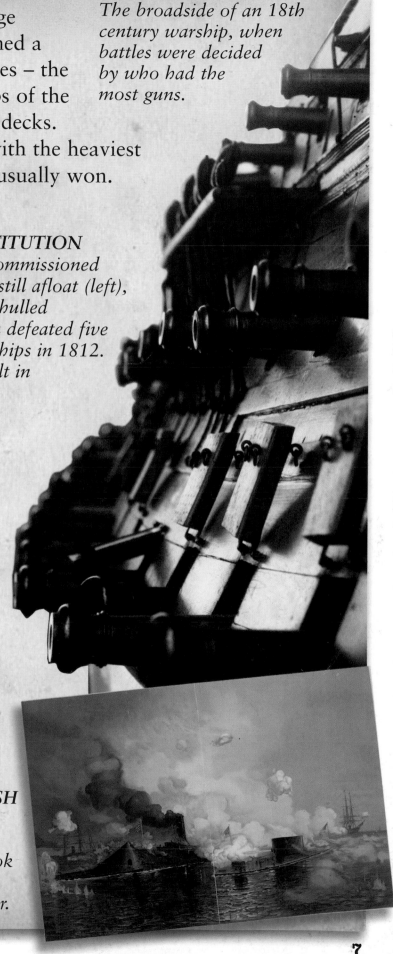

BROADSIDE
The broadside of an 18th century warship, when battles were decided by who had the most guns.

USS CONSTITUTION
The oldest commissioned naval vessel still afloat (left), the wooden hulled Constitution defeated five British warships in 1812. She was built in the 1790s.

STEAM AND STEEL

From the mid 19th century, the sailing ships of the line were replaced by metal-hulled, steam-powered battleships, while the sailing frigates were replaced by steam-powered cruisers. With the invention of rotating turrets, the guns could be aimed independently of the direction of the ship.

ARMOURED CRUISER
Launched in 1887, Dupuy de Lôme was a forerunner of the 20th century dreadnoughts.

IRONCLAD CLASH
The first proper battle between armoured ships took place during the American Civil War.

SEA POWER

In 1904, Britain's First Sea Lord, Sir John Fisher, was convinced of the need for fast, powerful ships. Fisher's concern was the submarines and destroyers, equipped with torpedoes, that had a greater range than battleship guns.

DREADNOUGHTS AND CARRIERS

Fisher's answer was the battlecruiser Dreadnought, heavily armed with ten 305 millimetre guns and the first warship to be propelled to 21 knots (39 km/h) by steam turbines. During World War I, however, the great dreadnought fleets were less effective than expected, as the threats to battleships from submarines, mines and torpedoes were too great without protection from destroyers. With the invention of fixed wing aircraft in 1903, navies were soon launching planes from warships.

BRANDTAUCHER
Brandtaucher was a German submersible built in 1850 – one of the first military submarines.

U-BOAT
By 1918, thousands of tons of Allied shipping had been sunk by the German U-boats during World War I.

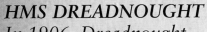

HMS DREADNOUGHT
In 1906, Dreadnought (above) revolutionised naval power. The resulting arms race created monsters like USS Texas, built in 1912 (right).

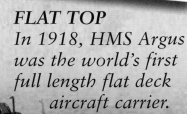

FLAT TOP
In 1918, HMS Argus was the world's first full length flat deck aircraft carrier.

BISMARCK
Perhaps the most famous ship of World War II, Bismarck was ultimately defeated by carrier borne aircraft.

LAST GREAT NAVAL WAR

By the beginning of World War II, it had become clear that aircraft carriers were the leading ships of the fleet and that battleships now performed a secondary role. The Battle of the Atlantic was fought between destroyers and submarines, and most of the decisive fleet clashes of the Pacific war were determined by aircraft carriers.

USS FORRESTAL
This 1950s ship was one of the first carriers to feature an angled landing deck with a straight take-off deck.

MODERN NAVIES

Modern warships are generally divided into seven main categories, which are: aircraft carriers, cruisers, destroyers, frigates, corvettes, submarines and amphibious assault craft. Each category has its own role in a modern navy.

TYPHOON
This Soviet ballistic missile launcher was the largest class of submarine ever built.

TICONDEROGA
The US Ticonderoga class cruiser (right) is a typical modern warship using guided missiles rather than guns for its main armament.

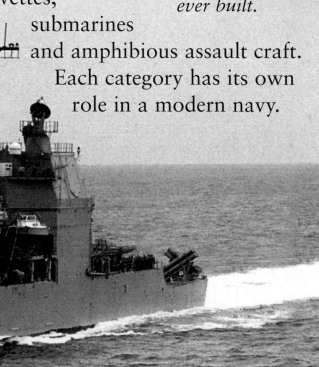

BALLISTIC MISSILE SUBMARINE

Ballistic missile submarines are equipped to launch long-range, rocket-powered missiles. These massive submarines prowl the ocean depths as moveable missile platforms, keeping as quiet as possible. They have two crews, Blue and Gold, with each crew on duty for a 100-day shift.

SAIL/FIN

The sail or fin houses the conning tower, the periscopes, radar and communications masts (antenna). It may also support control surfaces which are used for underwater stability and steering.

SLBM (Submarine-Launched Ballistic Missile)

Periscope

Radar and radio antennae

Launch hatch

Control surface

Control room

Periscope

Water filled nose cone

Crew quarters

Torpedo tubes

SONAR

For most of the time the submarine uses passive sonar to listen for the enemy. Active sonar sends out pulses of sound which would give away the submarine's position.

CONTROL ROOM

In this large, well-lit room are the controls for most of the sub's vital operations including periscopes, navigation (which uses GPS – Global Positioning System), large plotting tables, steering, ballast control and weapons control.

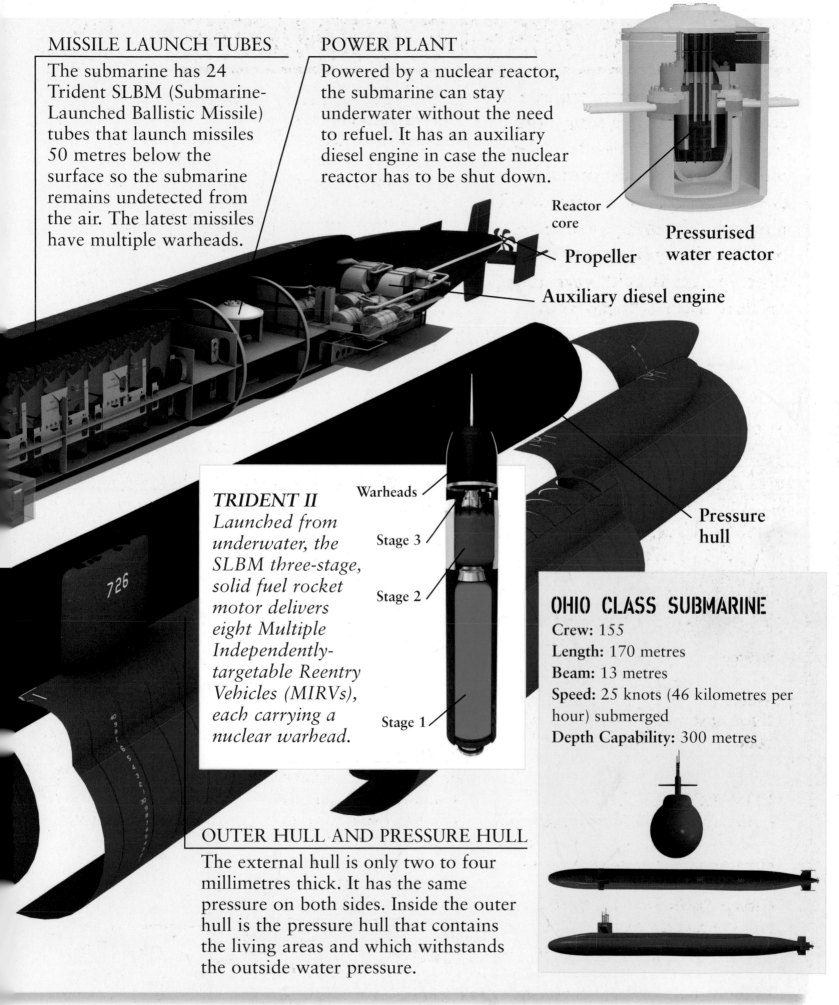

MISSILE LAUNCH TUBES

The submarine has 24 Trident SLBM (Submarine-Launched Ballistic Missile) tubes that launch missiles 50 metres below the surface so the submarine remains undetected from the air. The latest missiles have multiple warheads.

POWER PLANT

Powered by a nuclear reactor, the submarine can stay underwater without the need to refuel. It has an auxiliary diesel engine in case the nuclear reactor has to be shut down.

Reactor core

Propeller

Pressurised water reactor

Auxiliary diesel engine

Pressure hull

TRIDENT II

Launched from underwater, the SLBM three-stage, solid fuel rocket motor delivers eight Multiple Independently-targetable Reentry Vehicles (MIRVs), each carrying a nuclear warhead.

Warheads

Stage 3

Stage 2

Stage 1

OHIO CLASS SUBMARINE

Crew: 155
Length: 170 metres
Beam: 13 metres
Speed: 25 knots (46 kilometres per hour) submerged
Depth Capability: 300 metres

OUTER HULL AND PRESSURE HULL

The external hull is only two to four millimetres thick. It has the same pressure on both sides. Inside the outer hull is the pressure hull that contains the living areas and which withstands the outside water pressure.

FAST ATTACK SUBMARINE

These nuclear-powered submarines seek and destroy enemy submarines and surface ships. They can also attack targets on land with Tomahawk cruise missiles, carry Special Operation Forces, perform Intelligence, Surveillance and Reconnaissance (ISR) missions and engage in mine warfare.

LOS ANGELES CLASS SUBMARINE

Crew: 127
Length: 110 metres
Beam: 10 metres
Top speed: 33 knots (61 kilometres per hour) submerged
Depth Capability: 290 metres

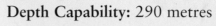

MULTIPLE LAUNCH TUBES

12 Vertical Launch System tubes fire the Tomahawk cruise missiles. Ejected by gas pressure, the missiles exit the water and a rocket is ignited for the first few seconds of airborne flight until the wings unfold and the turbofan engine can be used.

Sonar

Turbofan engine

Wings

Airscoop

Tomahawk cruise missile

TORPEDO TUBES

Torpedoes, anti-ship missiles and even Tomahawk cruise missiles can all be launched from the torpedo tubes.

CRUISE MISSILE

The missile's wings unfold for flight, the airscoop is exposed and the turbofan engine is employed for cruising. Over water, the Tomahawk uses inertial guidance or GPS to follow a preset course.

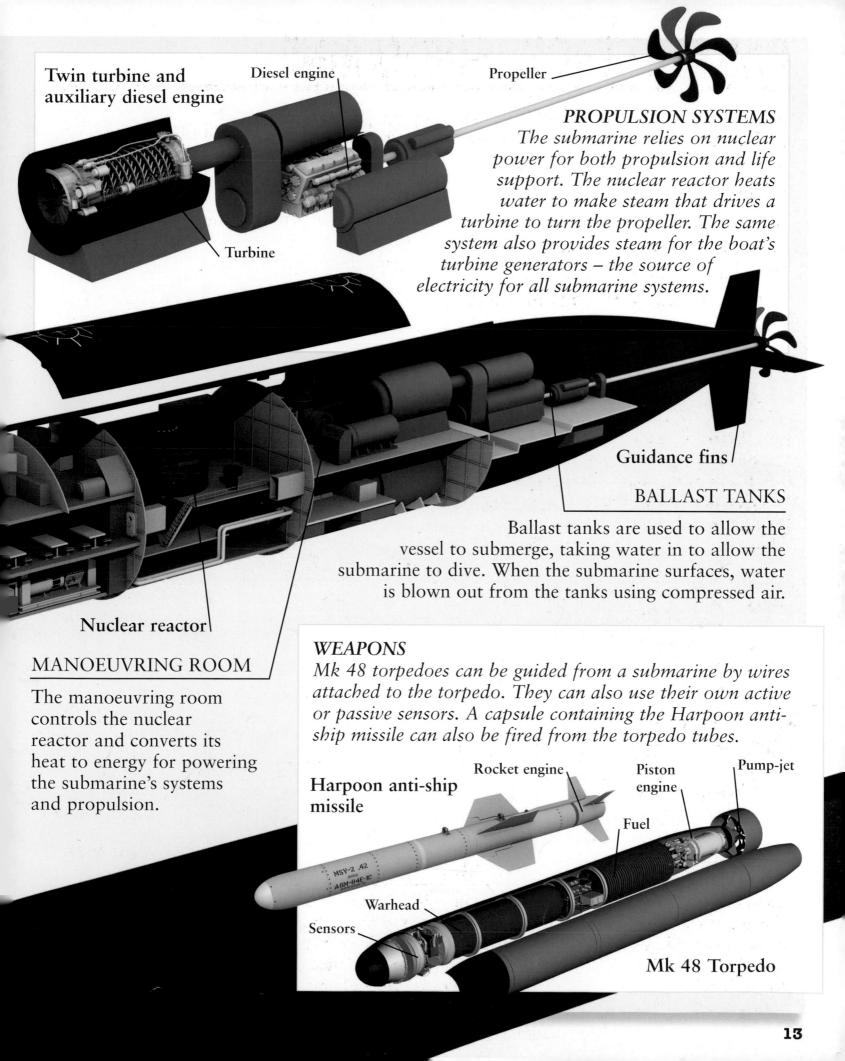

Twin turbine and auxiliary diesel engine

Diesel engine

Propeller

Turbine

PROPULSION SYSTEMS

The submarine relies on nuclear power for both propulsion and life support. The nuclear reactor heats water to make steam that drives a turbine to turn the propeller. The same system also provides steam for the boat's turbine generators – the source of electricity for all submarine systems.

Guidance fins

BALLAST TANKS

Ballast tanks are used to allow the vessel to submerge, taking water in to allow the submarine to dive. When the submarine surfaces, water is blown out from the tanks using compressed air.

Nuclear reactor

MANOEUVRING ROOM

The manoeuvring room controls the nuclear reactor and converts its heat to energy for powering the submarine's systems and propulsion.

WEAPONS

Mk 48 torpedoes can be guided from a submarine by wires attached to the torpedo. They can also use their own active or passive sensors. A capsule containing the Harpoon anti-ship missile can also be fired from the torpedo tubes.

Harpoon anti-ship missile

Rocket engine

Piston engine

Pump-jet

Fuel

MSV-2 42
AGM-84E-IC

Warhead

Sensors

Mk 48 Torpedo

DIESEL-ELECTRIC SUBMARINE

A diesel-electric submarine is a highly advanced non-nuclear submarine. It can operate at high speed on diesel power or switch to an electric-powered system for silent, slow cruising, staying submerged for up to three weeks.

CONTROL ROOM
Command and weapons control systems are monitored along with sensors, weapons and navigation.

LIVING QUARTERS
The area where the crew sleeps and eats is cramped. Every small space is used for storage.

Sail

Main sonar

Batteries

Torpedo tubes

WEAPONS
There are six torpedo tubes in two groups of three. The Type 212 submarine uses a water ram expulsion system for launching torpedoes such as the Black Shark heavyweight torpedo, which has fibre-optic wire guidance. The short range IDAS missile is being developed to fire from 212's torpedo tubes.

IDAS (Interactive Defence and Attack System) missile

Black Shark heavy torpedo

TOWED SONAR ARRAY

Sonar devices can be towed behind a submarine to listen for enemy ships and submarines, so they have less interference from the noise of the submarine.

Oxygen supply

ACTAS sonar

Stabiliser fins

TYPE 212 U-BOAT

Crew: 23-27
Length: 56 metres
Beam: 7 metres
Top speed: 20 knots (37 kilometres per hour) submerged
Depth Capability: over 700 metres

OUTER HULL

On modern military submarines the outer hull is covered with a layer of sound-absorbing rubber to reduce detection.

Prop motor

Hydrogen

PROPULSION SYSTEMS

The Type 212 is propelled by a diesel engine and an additional Air-Independent Propulsion (AIP) system which uses hydrogen fuel cells. Stored in tanks between the pressure hull and outer light hull, the hydrogen and oxidiser are piped through the pressure hull to the fuel cells when electricity is needed. The fuel cell system has nine fuel cells, each of which provides between 30 and 50 kilowatts of electricity.

Combination diesel or fuel cell/electric system

Oxygen

Fuel cells

Diesel engine

Propeller

Hydrogen

Fuel cells

Diesel generator

Outer hull

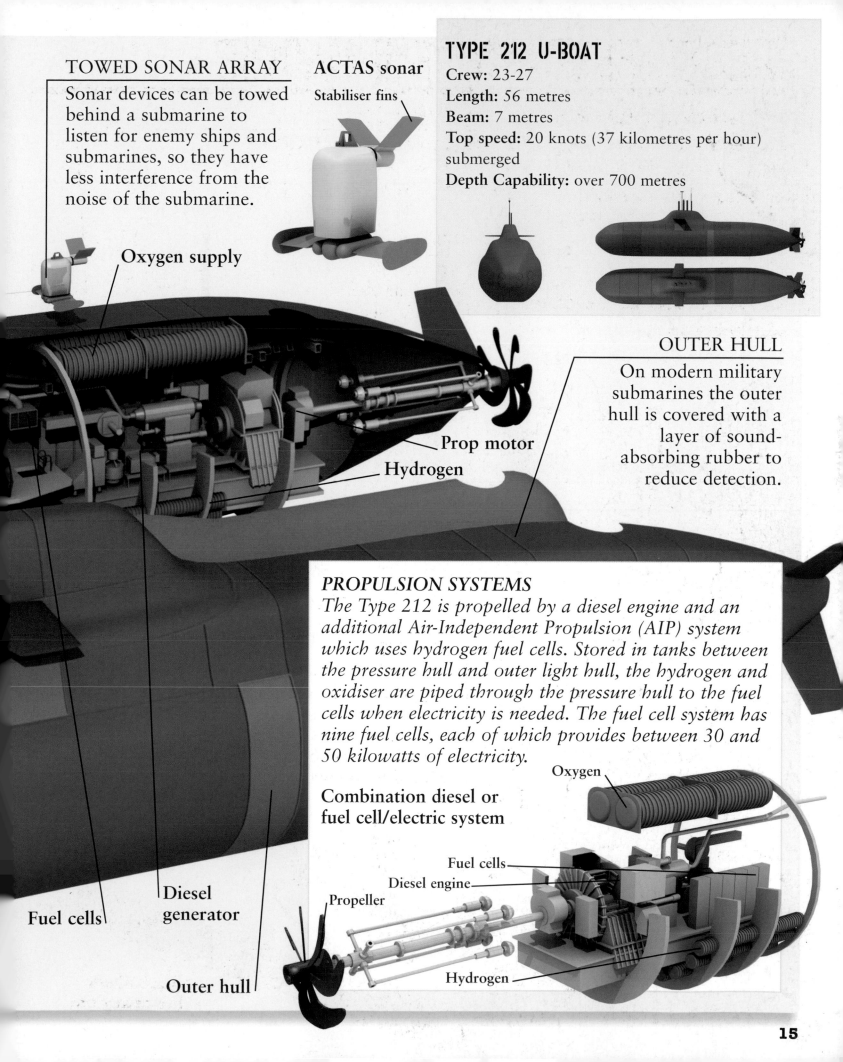

AIRCRAFT CARRIER

Aircraft carriers allow a naval force to provide air power at great distances without having to depend on land bases. The Nimitz-class supercarriers, a line of nuclear-powered aircraft carriers in service with the US Navy, are the largest warships in the world. Each displaces over 100,000 tonnes fully loaded.

Nose gear

Deck

Track

Piston

Catapult steam vessel

CATAPULT

Powerful steam catapults (known as 'Fat Cats') launch 37-tonne jets from zero to a speed of up to 289 km/h in under three seconds, across a distance of 91 metres. A track is built into the flight deck, below which is a large piston or shuttle that is attached through the track to the nose gear of the aircraft.

FLIGHT DECK

The flight deck is divided into two runways. One, with a catapult, is for take-off, the other, at an angle, is for landing.

CREW QUARTERS

About 60 personnel share a compartment, sleeping in single bunks, called racks, built together in stacks of three.

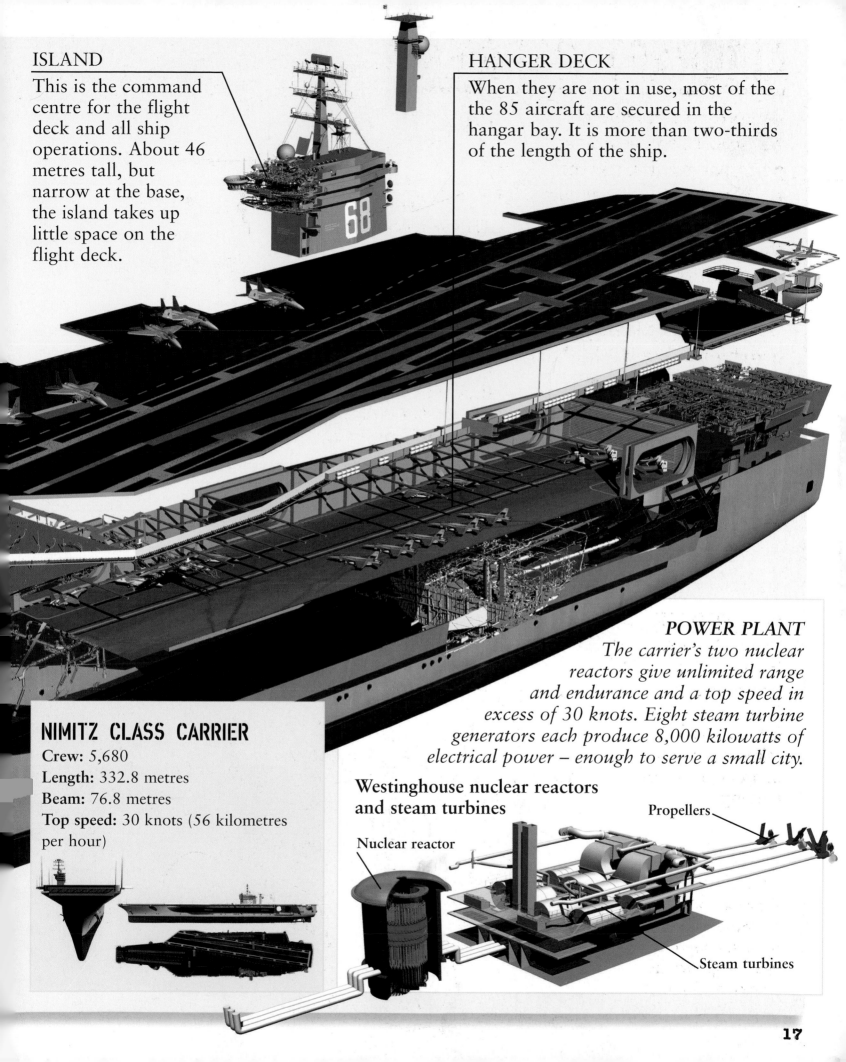

ISLAND

This is the command centre for the flight deck and all ship operations. About 46 metres tall, but narrow at the base, the island takes up little space on the flight deck.

HANGER DECK

When they are not in use, most of the 85 aircraft are secured in the hangar bay. It is more than two-thirds of the length of the ship.

POWER PLANT

The carrier's two nuclear reactors give unlimited range and endurance and a top speed in excess of 30 knots. Eight steam turbine generators each produce 8,000 kilowatts of electrical power – enough to serve a small city.

Westinghouse nuclear reactors and steam turbines

Nuclear reactor

Propellers

Steam turbines

NIMITZ CLASS CARRIER

Crew: 5,680
Length: 332.8 metres
Beam: 76.8 metres
Top speed: 30 knots (56 kilometres per hour)

CRUISER

The Kirov class cruisers are the largest and most powerful warships in the Russian Navy, second only to aircraft carriers. Similar in size to a World War I battleship, they are referred to as large missile cruisers by the Russian Navy. Commissioned in the 1980s, only four were completed.

KIROV CLASS CRUISER ADMIRAL NAKHIMOV

Crew: 727
Length: 252 metres
Beam: 28.5 metres
Top speed: 30 knots
(56 kilometres per hour)

CRUISE MISSILE LAUNCHERS

The main weapons are 20 Shipwreck cruise missiles, which are mounted on deck and designed to engage enemy warships, and Snowstorm anti-sub missiles.

Shipwreck cruise missile

SAM 9 launchers

Hull bulb

Waterline

AIR DEFENCE MISSILES

12 launchers and 96 vertical launch air defence missiles can engage both air and surface targets.

HULL

The size of the ship means there is plenty of space for command, control and communications.

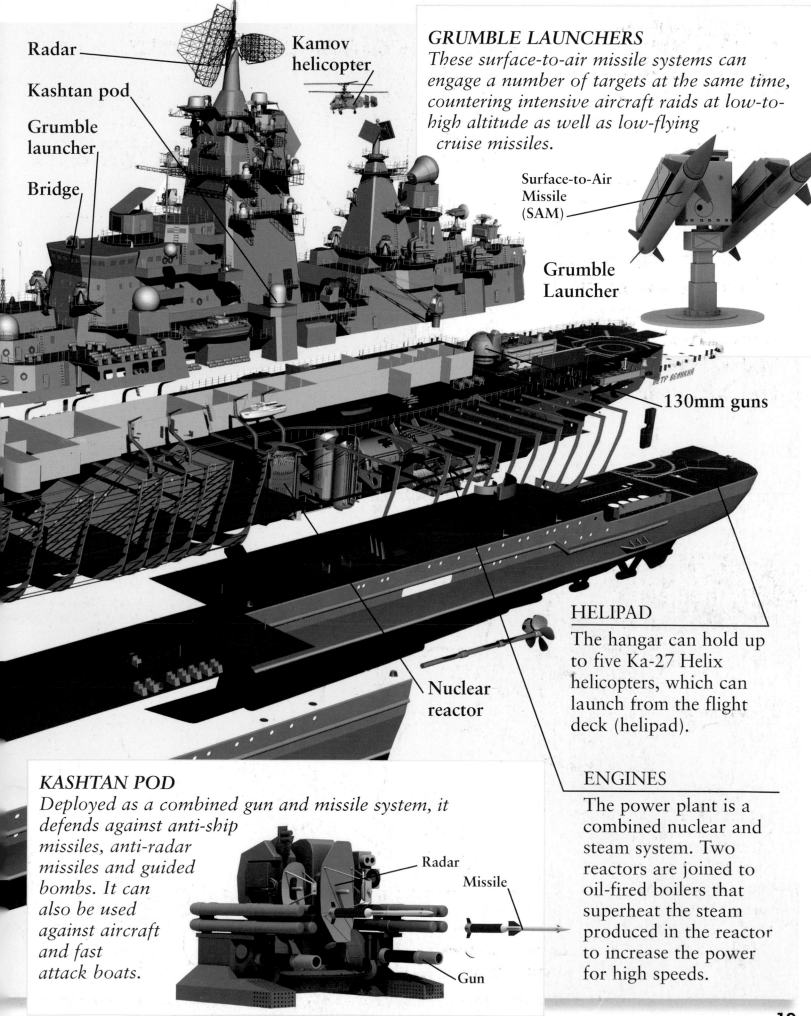

Radar

Kamov helicopter

Kashtan pod

Grumble launcher

Bridge

GRUMBLE LAUNCHERS
These surface-to-air missile systems can engage a number of targets at the same time, countering intensive aircraft raids at low-to-high altitude as well as low-flying cruise missiles.

Surface-to-Air Missile (SAM)

Grumble Launcher

130mm guns

HELIPAD
The hangar can hold up to five Ka-27 Helix helicopters, which can launch from the flight deck (helipad).

Nuclear reactor

KASHTAN POD
Deployed as a combined gun and missile system, it defends against anti-ship missiles, anti-radar missiles and guided bombs. It can also be used against aircraft and fast attack boats.

Radar

Missile

Gun

ENGINES
The power plant is a combined nuclear and steam system. Two reactors are joined to oil-fired boilers that superheat the steam produced in the reactor to increase the power for high speeds.

19

DESTROYER

Also known as guided missile destroyers, the main role of modern destroyers is to protect larger vessels, such as aircraft carriers, from attacks by aircraft. Other operational jobs range from humanitarian relief to anti-drug and embargo operations. Frigates have a similar job but specialise in anti-ship and anti-submarine warfare.

MULTI-FUNCTION RADAR

To perform its role the destroyer relies on a sophisticated radar system. The Samson multi-function radar system detects all types of targets to a distance of 400 kilometres. Able to track hundreds of targets at once, it is virtually immune to enemy jamming.

Long distance radar

Samson radar

Lynx helicopter

Crew bunks

30mm gun

Mess area

ENGINES

The huge amount of electricity used by the ship's systems, and two electric propulsion motors, is supplied by two gas turbines.

CREW AREAS

Cabins, messes and recreational areas are suitable for male and female sailors. There is also space to board 60 Royal Marines and their equipment.

BRIDGE

All ship operations are commanded from here.

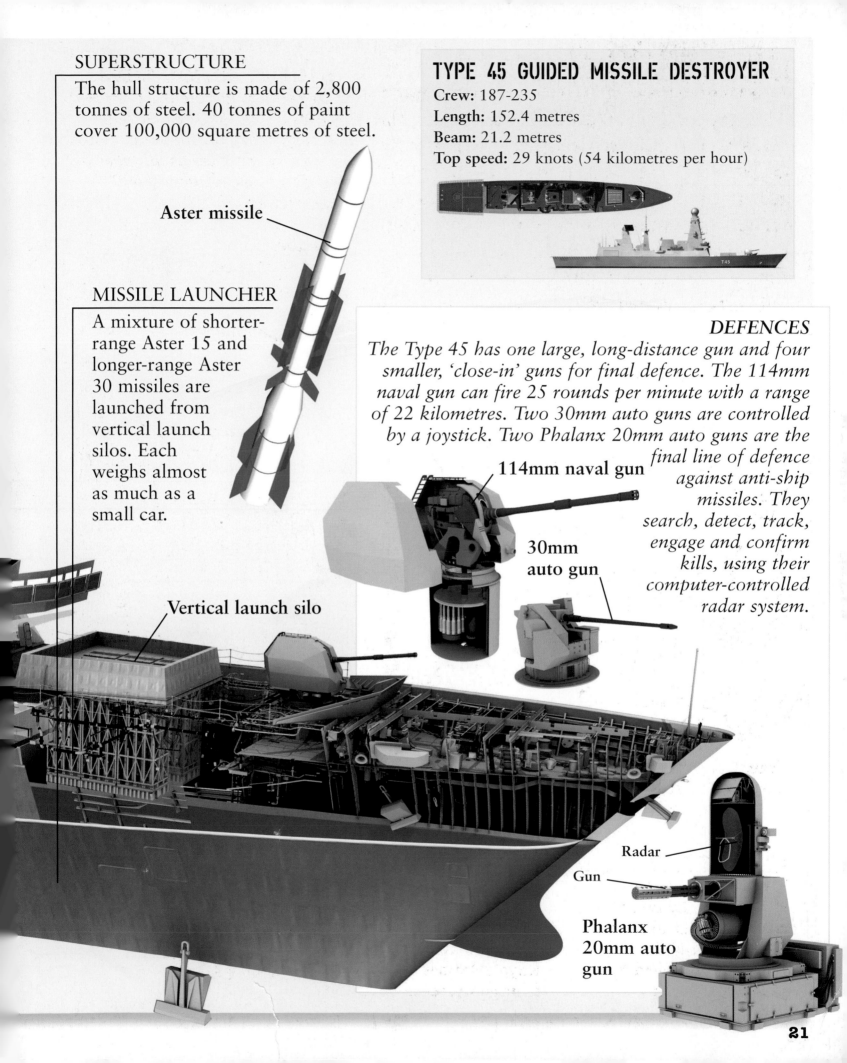

SUPERSTRUCTURE

The hull structure is made of 2,800 tonnes of steel. 40 tonnes of paint cover 100,000 square metres of steel.

Aster missile

MISSILE LAUNCHER

A mixture of shorter-range Aster 15 and longer-range Aster 30 missiles are launched from vertical launch silos. Each weighs almost as much as a small car.

Vertical launch silo

TYPE 45 GUIDED MISSILE DESTROYER

Crew: 187-235
Length: 152.4 metres
Beam: 21.2 metres
Top speed: 29 knots (54 kilometres per hour)

DEFENCES

The Type 45 has one large, long-distance gun and four smaller, 'close-in' guns for final defence. The 114mm naval gun can fire 25 rounds per minute with a range of 22 kilometres. Two 30mm auto guns are controlled by a joystick. Two Phalanx 20mm auto guns are the final line of defence against anti-ship missiles. They search, detect, track, engage and confirm kills, using their computer-controlled radar system.

114mm naval gun

30mm auto gun

Radar

Gun

Phalanx 20mm auto gun

STEALTH CORVETTE

Corvettes are small, manoeuvrable, lightly armed warships. The Visby is the latest class of corvette to be adopted by the Swedish Navy. The Visby's angular design uses stealth technology to create a 'low visibility' presence and its reduced radar signature gives an advantage over enemy ships. All Visby's functions can be hidden behind panels to enable it to keep the smoothest shape possible.

57MM BOFORS GUN

This automatic gun fires up to 220 rounds a minute. The barrel is fully retracted inside the gun casing to reduce its radar signature when not in use.

Pop-up weapons director

ASW grenade launchers

Bow thrusters

WEAPONS

The Visby uses sea skimming, 'fire and forget' missiles, fired from concealed launchers. Anti-Submarine Warfare (ASW) capability includes homing torpedoes launched from fixed tubes in the stern. The Visby also carries grenades and depth charges.

RBS 15 Mk II anti-ship missile

Computer guidance

Warhead

Turbojet engine

400mm anti-sub torpedo

Propeller

HULL

The hull is made of layers of carbon fibre and vinyl around a plastic core. This material is strong but light, provides good shock resistance and has a low radar signature.

VISBY CLASS CORVETTE

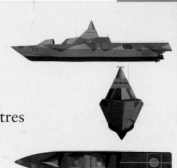

Crew: 43
Length: 72.6 metres
Beam: 10.4 metres
Top speed: 40 knots (87 kilometres per hour)

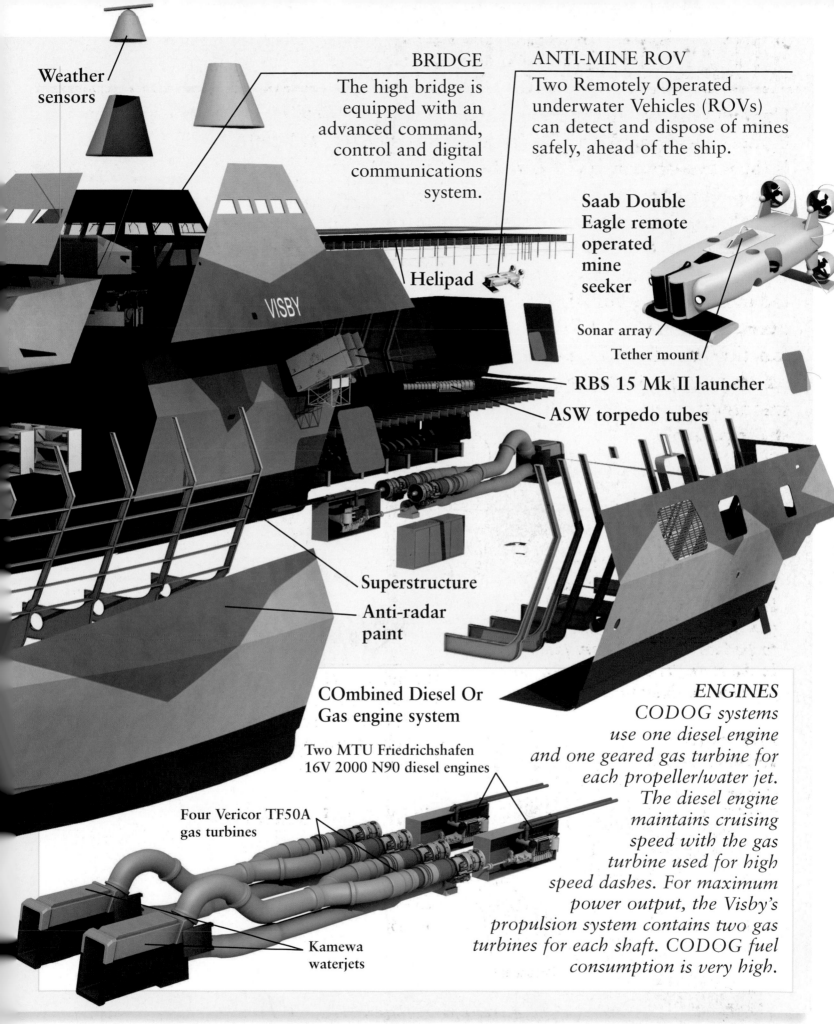

Weather sensors

BRIDGE
The high bridge is equipped with an advanced command, control and digital communications system.

ANTI-MINE ROV
Two Remotely Operated underwater Vehicles (ROVs) can detect and dispose of mines safely, ahead of the ship.

VISBY

Helipad

Saab Double Eagle remote operated mine seeker

Sonar array

Tether mount

RBS 15 Mk II launcher

ASW torpedo tubes

Superstructure

Anti-radar paint

COmbined Diesel Or Gas engine system

Two MTU Friedrichshafen 16V 2000 N90 diesel engines

Four Vericor TF50A gas turbines

Kamewa waterjets

ENGINES
CODOG systems use one diesel engine and one geared gas turbine for each propeller/water jet. The diesel engine maintains cruising speed with the gas turbine used for high speed dashes. For maximum power output, the Visby's propulsion system contains two gas turbines for each shaft. CODOG fuel consumption is very high.

LITTORAL COMBAT SHIP

Littoral Combat Ships (LCS) are small surface vessels that operate in the littoral zone (close to shore). Equipped with a flight deck and hangar space for two Seahawk helicopters, they are used as an assault transport. They can recover and launch small boats from a stern ramp and have enough cargo volume to deliver an assault force with armoured vehicles.

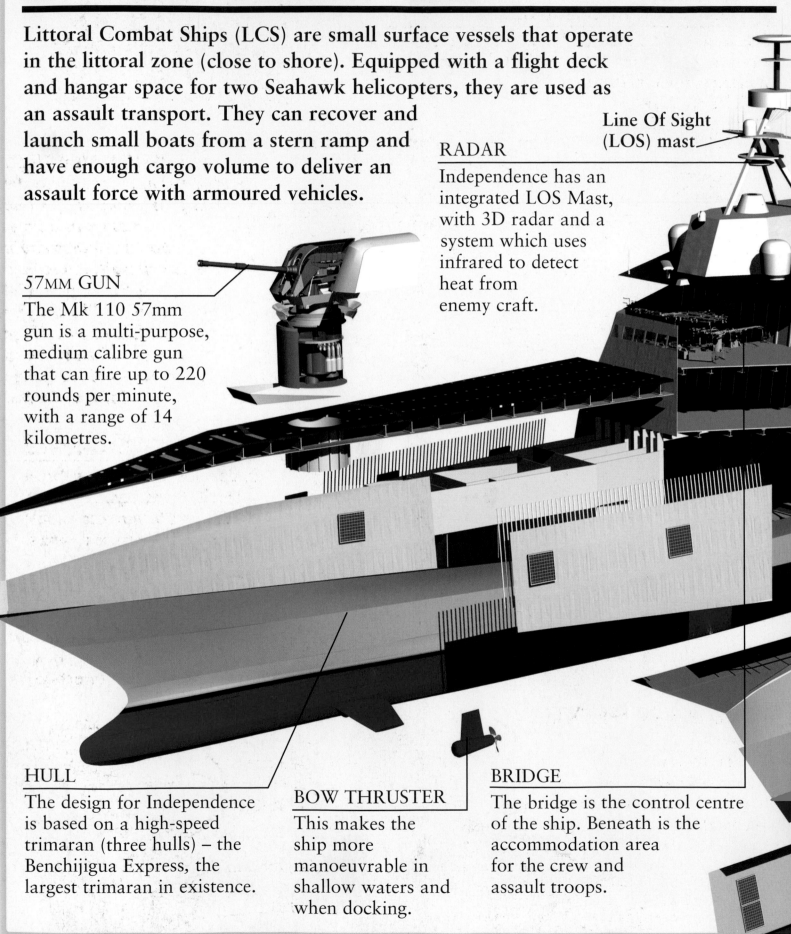

Line Of Sight (LOS) mast

RADAR
Independence has an integrated LOS Mast, with 3D radar and a system which uses infrared to detect heat from enemy craft.

57MM GUN
The Mk 110 57mm gun is a multi-purpose, medium calibre gun that can fire up to 220 rounds per minute, with a range of 14 kilometres.

HULL
The design for Independence is based on a high-speed trimaran (three hulls) – the Benchijigua Express, the largest trimaran in existence.

BOW THRUSTER
This makes the ship more manoeuvrable in shallow waters and when docking.

BRIDGE
The bridge is the control centre of the ship. Beneath is the accommodation area for the crew and assault troops.

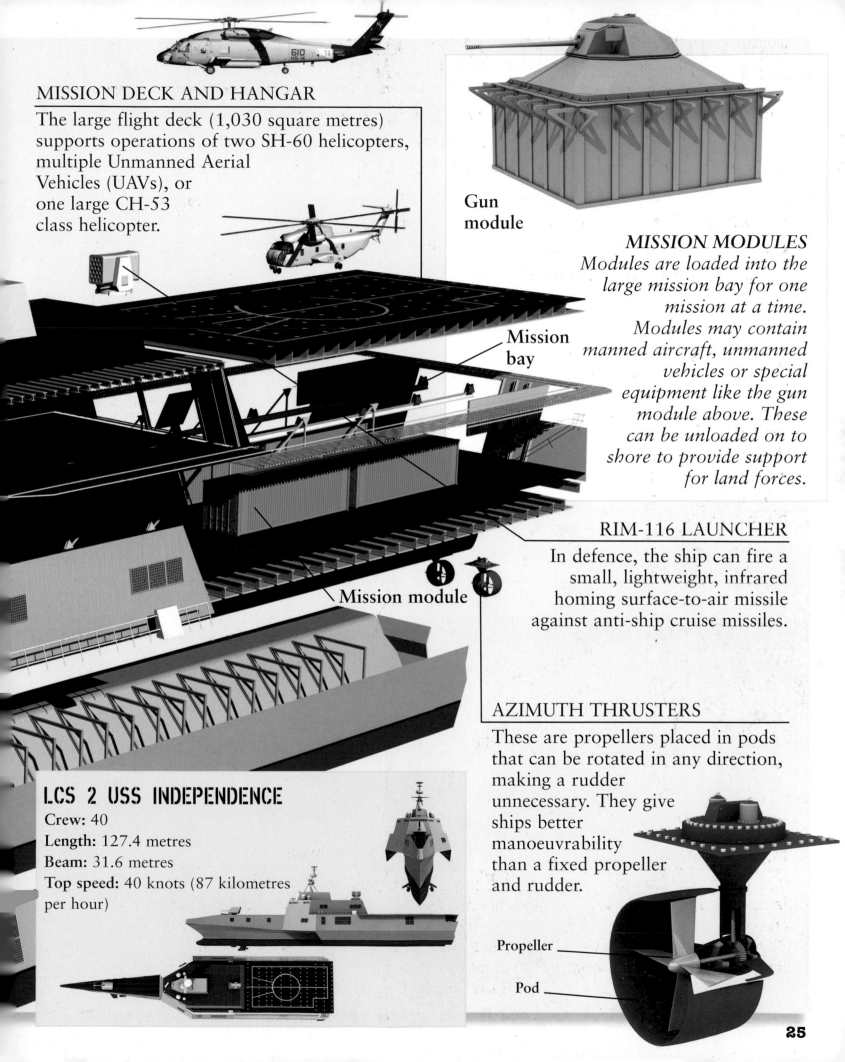

MISSION DECK AND HANGAR

The large flight deck (1,030 square metres) supports operations of two SH-60 helicopters, multiple Unmanned Aerial Vehicles (UAVs), or one large CH-53 class helicopter.

Gun module

Mission bay

Mission module

MISSION MODULES

Modules are loaded into the large mission bay for one mission at a time. Modules may contain manned aircraft, unmanned vehicles or special equipment like the gun module above. These can be unloaded on to shore to provide support for land forces.

RIM-116 LAUNCHER

In defence, the ship can fire a small, lightweight, infrared homing surface-to-air missile against anti-ship cruise missiles.

AZIMUTH THRUSTERS

These are propellers placed in pods that can be rotated in any direction, making a rudder unnecessary. They give ships better manoeuvrability than a fixed propeller and rudder.

Propeller

Pod

LCS 2 USS INDEPENDENCE

Crew: 40
Length: 127.4 metres
Beam: 31.6 metres
Top speed: 40 knots (87 kilometres per hour)

AMPHIBIOUS ASSAULT CRAFT

These high-speed, specialist craft are designed to sealift landing assault units, such as marines and tanks, from ships to shore, as well as to transport and plant mines. They are amphibious, meaning that they can travel over water or across beaches, and even go over walls up to 1.6 metres high.

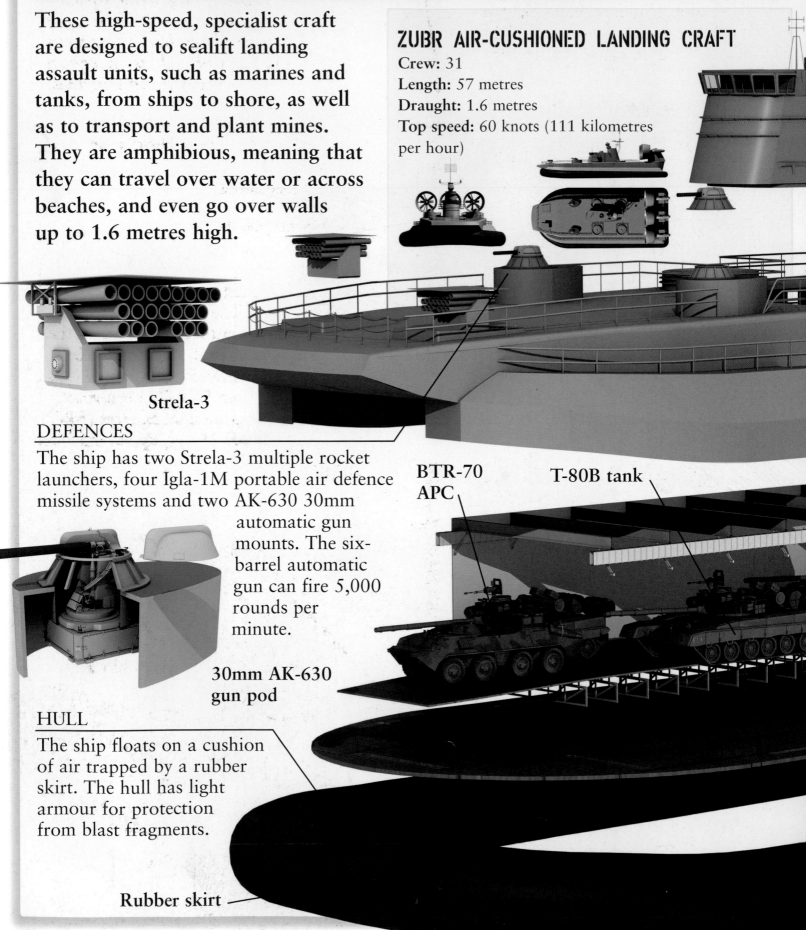

ZUBR AIR-CUSHIONED LANDING CRAFT
Crew: 31
Length: 57 metres
Draught: 1.6 metres
Top speed: 60 knots (111 kilometres per hour)

Strela-3

DEFENCES
The ship has two Strela-3 multiple rocket launchers, four Igla-1M portable air defence missile systems and two AK-630 30mm automatic gun mounts. The six-barrel automatic gun can fire 5,000 rounds per minute.

30mm AK-630 gun pod

BTR-70 APC

T-80B tank

HULL
The ship floats on a cushion of air trapped by a rubber skirt. The hull has light armour for protection from blast fragments.

Rubber skirt

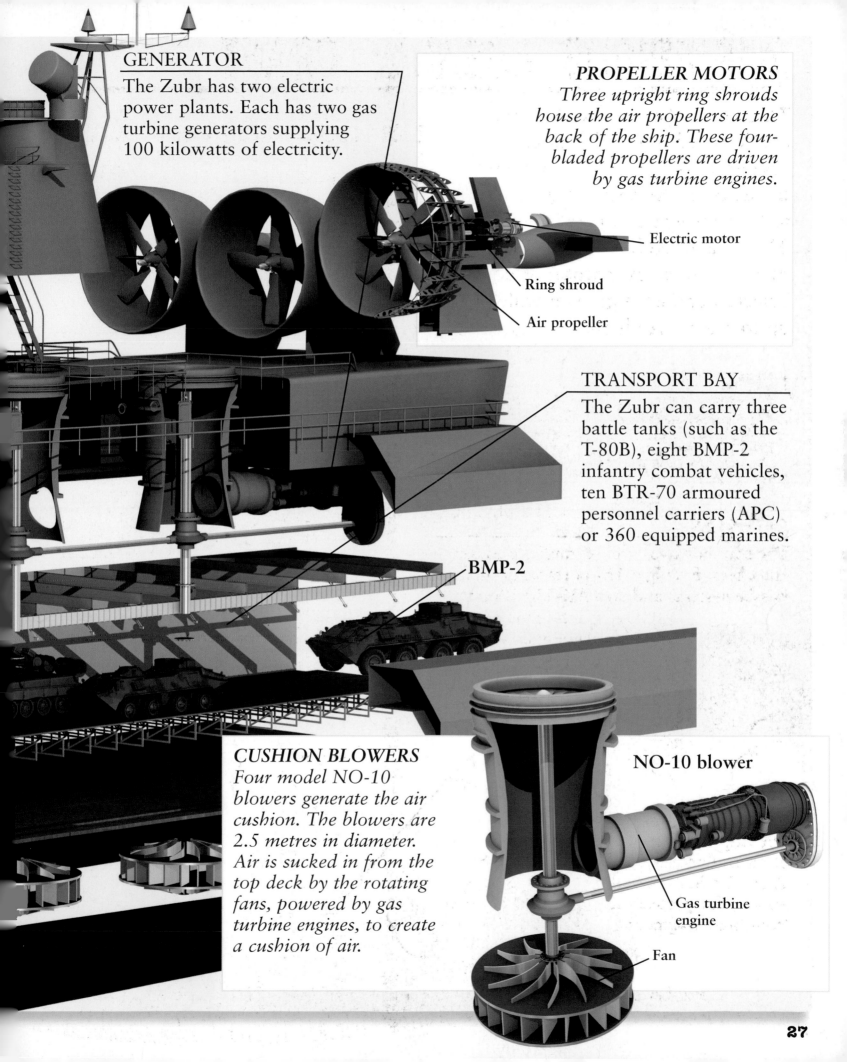

GENERATOR
The Zubr has two electric power plants. Each has two gas turbine generators supplying 100 kilowatts of electricity.

PROPELLER MOTORS
Three upright ring shrouds house the air propellers at the back of the ship. These four-bladed propellers are driven by gas turbine engines.

Electric motor

Ring shroud

Air propeller

TRANSPORT BAY
The Zubr can carry three battle tanks (such as the T-80B), eight BMP-2 infantry combat vehicles, ten BTR-70 armoured personnel carriers (APC) or 360 equipped marines.

BMP-2

CUSHION BLOWERS
Four model NO-10 blowers generate the air cushion. The blowers are 2.5 metres in diameter. Air is sucked in from the top deck by the rotating fans, powered by gas turbine engines, to create a cushion of air.

NO-10 blower

Gas turbine engine

Fan

MINE HUNTER-KILLER

These ships hunt out mines and destroy or neutralise them. Avenger class ships are mine hunter-killers capable of finding, classifying and destroying moored and bottom mines.

SONAR STATIONS

The ship uses sonar and video systems, cable cutters and a mine-detonating device which is monitored at the sonar stations.

AVENGER CLASS MINE COUNTERMEASURES SHIP

Crew: 84

Length: 68 metres

Beam: 12 metres

Top speed: 14 knots (25.76 kilometres per hour)

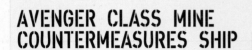

HULL AND SUPERSTRUCTURE

The hulls of the Avenger class ships are of wood with an external coat of fibreglass which gives the ship a low magnetic signature.

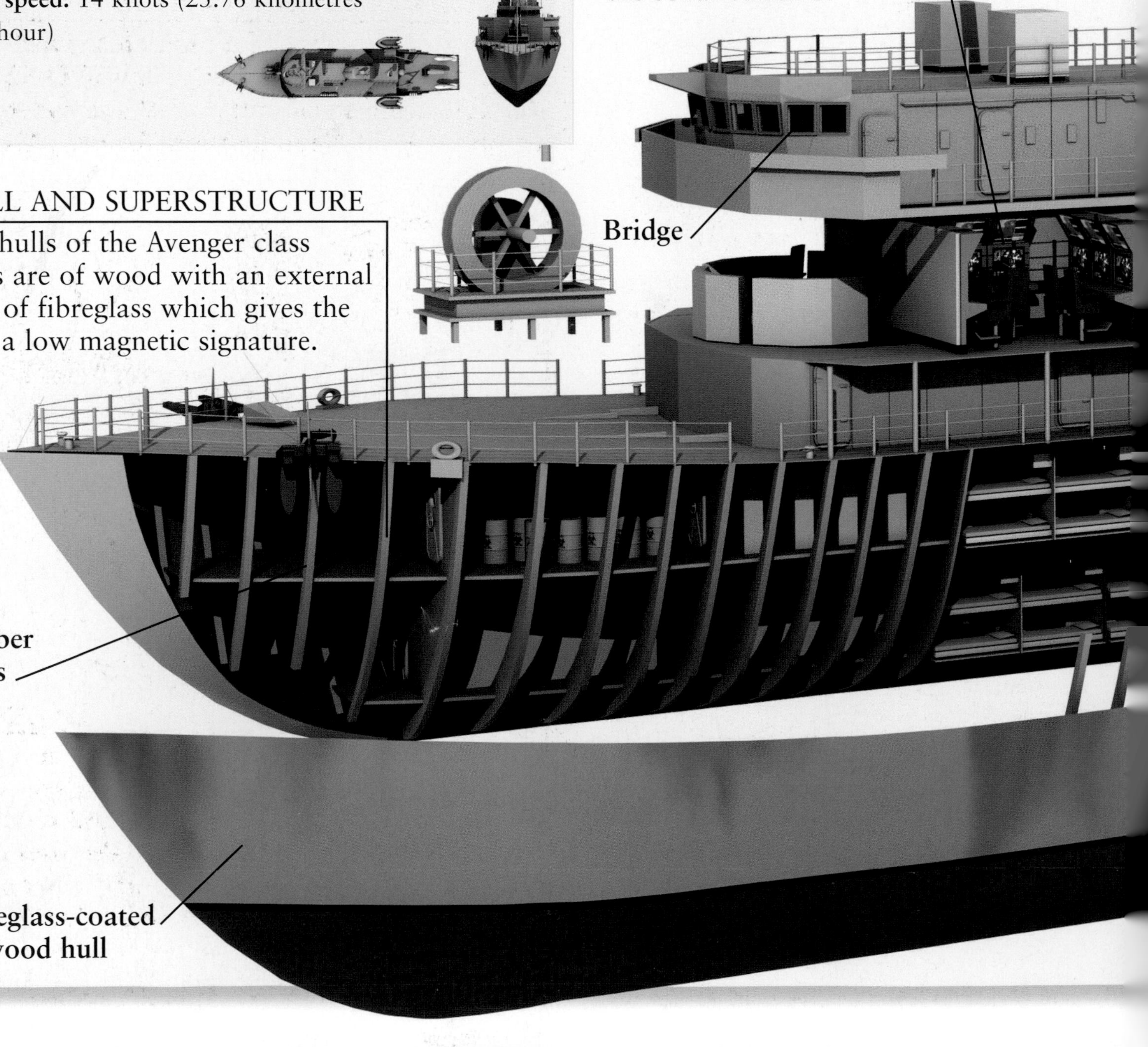

Bridge

Timber spars

Fibreglass-coated plywood hull

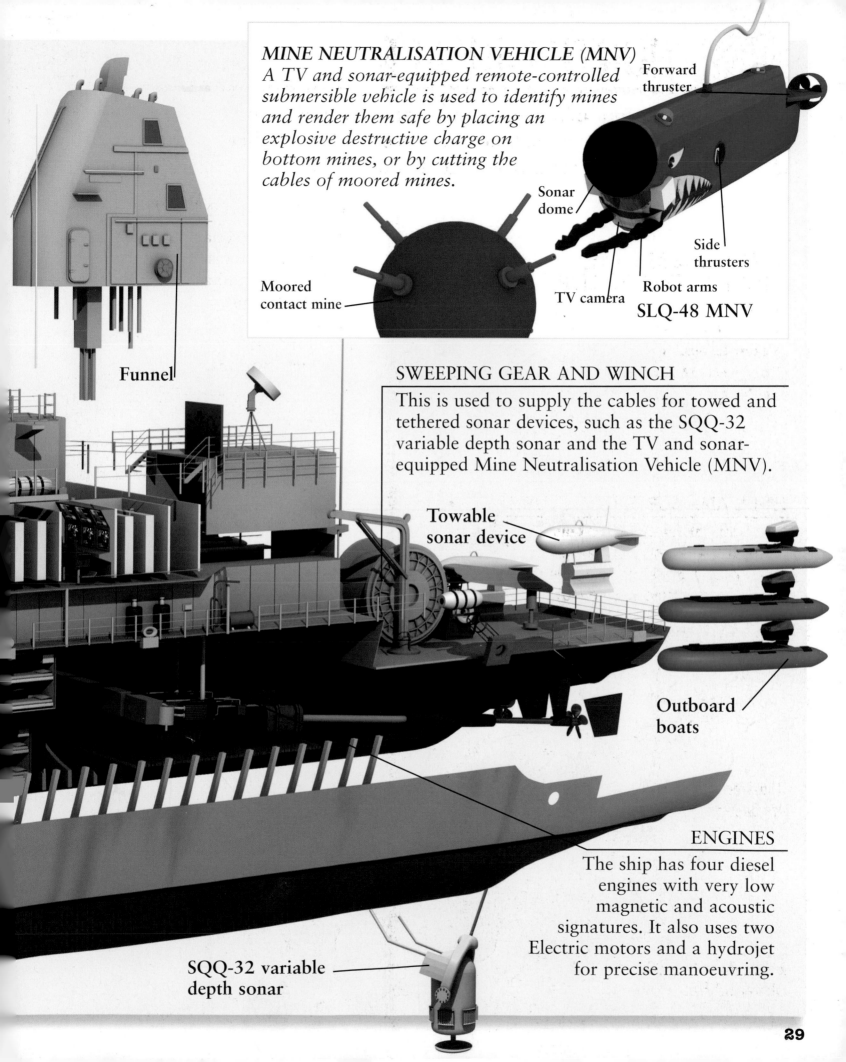

MINE NEUTRALISATION VEHICLE (MNV)

A TV and sonar-equipped remote-controlled submersible vehicle is used to identify mines and render them safe by placing an explosive destructive charge on bottom mines, or by cutting the cables of moored mines.

Forward thruster

Sonar dome

Side thrusters

Moored contact mine

TV camera

Robot arms

SLQ-48 MNV

Funnel

SWEEPING GEAR AND WINCH

This is used to supply the cables for towed and tethered sonar devices, such as the SQQ-32 variable depth sonar and the TV and sonar-equipped Mine Neutralisation Vehicle (MNV).

Towable sonar device

Outboard boats

ENGINES

The ship has four diesel engines with very low magnetic and acoustic signatures. It also uses two Electric motors and a hydrojet for precise manoeuvring.

SQQ-32 variable depth sonar

FUTURE MACHINES

In the future warships will differ fundamentally from today's vessels. They will be difficult to see due to anti-radar technology and difficult to hear because they will run on electric motors.

FUTURE SUPERCARRIER
The Gerald R. Ford class aircraft carriers will be easier to maintain and more efficient during their 50-year service life.

Future warships may well be engineered as modular vessels consisting of several zones. If one zone gets severely damaged in an attack, automatic controls will instantaneously reroute the power to the rest of the ship. They will look very different from the ships of today. Stealth technology requires no right angles in the design and all weapons will be hidden away beneath smooth surfaces.

USS FREEDOM
The prototype littoral combat ship USS Freedom (above) is an alternative design to the USS Independence (see p24–25).

ZUMWALT
An artist's rendering of the Zumwalt class destroyer, a new class of multi-mission US Navy surface combatant ship. It is forecast to be patrolling the seas by 2013.

GLOSSARY

ballistic missile
A missile that follows a curved flightpath to deliver a warhead (often nuclear) to an enemy target.

beam
The width of a ship at the widest point.

capital ship
The capital ships of a navy are its most important warships.

embargo
An official ban on trade with a particular country for political reasons.

fuel cell
A fuel cell produces electricity from a fuel such as hydrogen and oxygen.

GPS
Global Positioning System. A system of satellites that allows people with specialised receivers to pinpoint exactly where they are on the Earth.

inertial guidance
An electronic system that monitors position, speed and acceleration, to provide navigational information without communicating with a base station.

infrared
Part of the electromagnetic spectrum (like light rays), far infrared waves are thermal in the form of heat. Near infrared waves are shorter, not hot and used by many devices including TV remote controllers.

nuclear reactor
An enclosed vessel supplying an energy source for the generation of steam using controlled nuclear chain reactions.

RADAR
RADAR (RAdio Detection And Ranging) is an object detection system that uses electromagnetic waves to identify the range, altitude, direction and speed of objects such as aircraft, ships and missiles.

signature
The amount by which a ship or other craft registers in a detection system such as radar or infrared. A low or small signature means it is hardly detectable.

SONAR
SONAR (SOund Navigation And Ranging) is a technique that uses sound (usually underwater) to navigate, communicate with or detect other vessels. Active sonar sends out sounds and listens to the 'echo' while passive sonar only 'listens'.

stealth technology
Also known as LO (Low Observable), this technology aims to make military craft less visible (or invisible) to radar, infrared, sonar and other detection methods.

turbine
A rotary engine with blades that are turned at high speed by steam or other hot gases. The rotation can be used to turn propellers or to power a generator to produce electricity.

INDEX